As if Only

IAN DAVIDSON

As if Only

Shearsman Books
Exeter

Published in the United Kingdom in 2007 by
Shearsman Books Ltd
58 Velwell Road
Exeter EX4 4LD

ISBN-13   978-1-905700-08-0

ISBN-10   1-905700-08-3

Acknowledgments

Some of these poems have previously beeen published in the magazines *Big Bridge*,
Ecopoetics, *Fieralingue*, *Fire*, *Jacket*, *Orbis*, *Pages*, *Poetry Wales* and the anthologies
Lie of the Land and *Onsets*. *No Way Back* was published by West House Books as a
pamphlet. My thanks to the editors concerned. These poems would not have been
possible without the support of the Welsh Academy through its AHRC-funded
fellowship scheme. My thanks to them.

The publisher gratefully acknowledges financial assistance from
Arts Council England.

CONTENTS

Introduction

When the place runs out on you, either rushing through the broadband, slowly covered over by the rising sea or receding to a distant memory, then the only place left is the body. So I turned back on myself and picked over the marks on my skin. I photographed myself from close up. I lost weight and put it back on. I tried to find out how my insides worked. I started smoking again then gave it up, many times. I had to spend a week in hospital with a throat so swollen I could barely breathe, let alone eat or drink. So the poems are about the body, and the desire of the body to communicate with others, whether through the rustle of skin on skin or tapping the keyboard. They're about the way technologies keep people apart and bring them closer together.

These poems were written in Bangor, in north Wales, in Barcelona, in London, on the Baltic coast and in Fez and Marrakech. Despite the distances involved they are the result of a period of introspection and self-possession. Travel doesn't necessarily broaden the mind. In some cases only the long lines would do, and the language had to be chewed over, while in others, when the town was quiet and the blood had stopped pounding in my head, I could clip the tone and measure out the words a few at a time.

A lot happened in the two years in which these poems were written. There was a war, and there were bombs in London. There were things hardly possible to deal with, including the return of an imperialist and colonialist attitude that I thought was part of history and would never return in my lifetime. Some of that gets in the poems. But I was mainly interested in myself, and how I'd got the way I had. How the traces of a life had marked the skin.

Ian Davidson

As if Only

The Body Con

Coda

And as if it was only the lifting
Or the sheer state of material
And as if it was only the wave formed
Or the sternum's fold

Where the organs sit where the
Internal becomes entwined at the
Seat of emotion the peristaltic
Gesture of movement towards

The organic from
Half open air seeps into
The interior is
Corrugated and the emotions

Bump towards language across the
Ridges in the brow towards
The furrowed teeth
The clenched aorta

I.

Whatever I may feel inside whenever I feel cut off from
as if the word feel becomes another word or if the word feel
paired with the word feel lost its harmonic and the unpaired

Becomes the impaired as if one half has been removed and the
single hand flapping helplessly in the space left to itself

This is a full body scan apt to discover the slightest
imperfection in excess body hair or a muscle out of place

don't do casual
don't do glance

It was only a branch line a further frame of reference another
addition to the sum of human contact or the careful phrasing of
language left out cell touching cell and prisoners of desire your

breast beneath the single sheet I was moved imperceptibly as if
the friction of hands across skin and all the inner mechanics

Oxygen bubbling up in blood the lesser curvature of the
stomach the superior part of the duodenum the lesser moment
beneath the skin the fish hooks of the present, gift wrapped

and knotted with bows becomes a present from the past or the
anxiety of a disappearing future a matter of presentation or
oiled to perfection from the con to the conviction an issue of

Incapacity or the shrinking fear I add up the prose and cons watch
the grey surface of the water become turquoise behind pale pink of
cloud cover wipe the surface of the eye as if loneliness was

Meant to be you have created a surface that both attracts and repels
you have groomed yourself to the last tip of each strand of hair pulled
lashes from their origins and the heart still or the heart beats or the

Kidneys take a breather and the liver's silent shudder as it squeezes
and filters out you adjust your diet according to your strength of feeling
I fought back the emotion scared that my organisation would barely

Cope or equanimity permanently threatened and breath
control become ungoverned you picked at crisps dis
carded the salad went for maximum calories as if your

Breasts might swell to their origins or your skinny frame regain its
given shape. You are cont. you go on and

maybe the consequence of many large branches from
straight line geometry or even the curves of calculus unable
to explain organs crossing apparently out of scale. I dismantled a

Body it was an imperfect fit according
to the laws of sexual activity they began to reflect

mirror mirror
that's an order

When sliced across the middle she writhes and the hairs on her
face began to glow and her tongue could
simply twitch I mean he demonstrated

By means of colour photography that a mixmaster can cause considerable
confusion if applied incorrectly or simply to the wrong body part and
then in their sickness or emotion or sex or the recognition of the love con.

It is a question of scale, scales falling from the eyes until in the
enormity of the imprinted word cutting across the organism like a
stick of rock the arrangement becomes tortuous and twisted

2. Where Ideas Come From

Shaking hair again and creating desire from nowhere and
looking up with the light behind said where do ideas come from
and I indicated the area around my line of vision and spread open

My hands tore down the curtains until out into the night sky there
was everything laid bare and she looked at me again and I began to get
ideas and their shapes were like things that could not be named but I

Began to name them. I stared hard at the top left hand corner under which
all who pass
will love and love again and I disappeared and the ideas came as if

From asking why too many times until the question became so familiar
that the unmarked underside turns to face the sun or the clear skin is
transparent as if the fabric of existence was torn in many places

and think
where do ideas

Come from as a limb wormed its way past or a cure for the present the ribbons
and bows from the waist skin stretched across stomach muscles which
was where ideas came from or the empty head that twitches towards the

Text message nothing going down or coming up I'll contact someone so
that's where ideas come from an abbreviated text or a Glasgow kiss c u
Jimmy an idea in the world might be from the heart or a baby's

Body split down the centre through an abrasion of the ear via interference
how the screen divided and the one and the other or the synchronic shifting of
affection nor the first nor the last and when a body leaves a body turning

A fresh page then the insides rustle there's a readjustment of the digestive
system an acceptance of food the slow torture of the worm turning more
definition less breath the medium becomes porous as in streaming the

Loss of moisture from the inside out she held up her
skin he folded back said that's

Where ideas come from or he stroked the surface and said
here is an idea the sound of milk being loaded or the early
call I've no idea where ideas come from maybe the morning light

3.

When the cracks show it is easy to make poetry.
Dismantling a psyche painfully arranged by the creaking
machinery of lightweights takes merely a steady push or a few
carefully placed words. Between the cracks I insert the words
ripping pieces levering open by means of applied

strategy and the whys and wherefores. It continues although
stuttering slightly rocking and off guard. Escape when the chance
arises. The malice of a destruction worker knows no bounds he can pick
up the pieces of a discarded life an old fireplace a piece of wall paper a
feeling for an old friend the trace of residency and through the insertion of

no more than a short bar bring the gables tumbling those walls so
painfully constructed by idiot matter come rippling into dust and then
the organs are revealed. The organisation of the inner structure is laid
thread bare. What a micro skirt could only hint at what a stumble
on the steps or a quiet moment might simply pin drop between

the arrangement of fibres and then the twitching frog of an inside
and self righteousness can begin to assert itself through the rough
cast of a locality the heather on the hills the moon rising behind a
bank of cloud a mountain frozen into presence. I have no support
structures no failsafe no ground beneath my feet no decency

Controlling the Page

There were no fit words

the words bounced back
unfit for use

when addressed I respond well whatever

I want to write about loss
as if through the grammar of glass
I want to write about this much

Things out of all proportion
the distance between digits intimate beyond the body
and trying not to write anything down
and scared of the dark
I repeat catch phrases knocking them dead

Narratives provide evidence
of opposing thoughts
I do mind the steps
they disturb me
the moment in which failing to play the game
the play became mechanical geared into itself the
dispersion of heat across bearings

It was a stand up world
where nobody asks why
resisting the desire to communicate
eager to please
inhabited out of deficiency

This is my story, this is why I
am different, this is where I was

It is not a lifestyle choice
but a consequence I have not
eaten the fruits of my toil there were
hours never in or out of work never in or

out of work or the space a hand makes on another
body spread across the
back the belly and a capacity within
the spaces inside I never realised such
shallowness existed re-writing
a history for every new context this is
what has happened to me and with
each re-telling shrinking the margins of the
world pieces of flesh lopped off

Going to the dogs and never big enough
inside never space in a
shrunken head or a heart that hardly
beat and devoted to your own story
you told yourself a thousand times
I can't because out of all that is

hinge point

it was a hinge point one of those events where
the past began to close up on the future
it was a can of worms breaking out just
beneath the surface a cannot on every lip
we will or will do nothing I walked the streets
by day I travelled the elementary canal I trawled
the suds at the basin's edge it was nothing to do with
rational it was every thing on legs that crawled or
human values like laughter or time and place
I could live anywhere or with any one seems like

I have extracted the meat from the bone
I have developed curvature of the upper back
I am wrapping myself in skin

Letting in the Light

I.

wandering as a river might
the past nearby
with little time
the statutes of breathing
or how the northern light shines

why do you say these things why do
these things you do say these things

2.

beneath skin and under my
breath I whisper my mistakes

it was as if

this is the right place to be
whatever
filled with cigarettes
how can I be
outside his own body
well the mobile kicked in
and then the picture book

I cannot draw pictures with words
the image, so clear in my mind
becomes a trembling finger becomes
the writing pen the ghosts
of the past how I've turned on the
light it seems like a story I'm
telling myself as if it's not true
and then in the re-telling it turns
out to be true

3.

making shut eye keeping
an image clear not quite
tough enough not quite
in shape a style I couldn't
recognise a long
sentence ten to life

4.

there were rules within the cortex

on one side the system sits while on the
other a picture book

I learn how to write
I clench my fingers around the pencil
the writing body
writes the holes are
new the way the pain gets out
through the running blood
thick with tension through the
new holes I open my mouth and
try to speak I cover my eyes my ears
I clap my hand to my mouth smoke
drifts from between fingers

5.

trying to talk through the skin
I shudder, it must be me
think for yourself
work things out
the person
I am
does some
thing with a body I listen
I forget half the time
to listen to the words
to one side of the question
I try to peer through other's eyes
as if through mist
they appear back

6.

I insert the blade
just beneath the skin
I see the blood flow
numb all over
all over dumb
the words dry up the endless
list of explanation the
excuses a drift into silence
only the tobacco gets through
or strong drink or the silence
following

7.

shapes appear
seeking complexity
the simple line drawing blood
a shape of a heart
the drift of the blade on unmarked skin
crossing the tracks and trails

8.

take a few care
of few not a
care with you or
in recovery I keep
the airways clear
check for repulse

Sheet Music

1.
The process of the setting sun
pink of pink clouds
2 birds completely
minute by minute
by not there
not here
nor their

does a seagull
or borrow association

decisions are aesthetic

scissors, fabric

2.
white and still
under the skin
thoughts
rotten to the core
barren heart
reclaimed face
fenced in
all that domestic

toned

as I got closer it began to break up

in the eyes behind red rims

June and it's raining

handle on the flesh

people I know a people
drawn through circumstance
and waiting for someone

3.
if love never fails

from here to there
now to then
fighting like
this
fibre of the mind
for so much
and into certain
words

the untouchable
turbulent
in
secure
buildings crumble
houses echo

I was asleep and I had a folded sheet of paper in my hand folded as an
envelope and on unfolding a small pale card with a word on the downside.
I didn't know the word but I couldn't move and a person sat across the
room and all I had to do was lift a limb or two and pass the card the word
would unlock everything. But my muscles wouldn't pick up the bones
although my mind was clear as crystal and the small pale card with the
hidden word which would unlock everything

touch as strangers
without organisation
perspire
emerging as strangers
opening a plaza
of possibility

the word might have been love
it might have been two words
sprung from a vantage point

and if love is between people a
failure to properly
open out the folded sheet
to pass over the word
to coordinate the limbs

The alley way – Barcelona 2004

I understand compulsion

limbs simply carriers for veins

I comprehend obsession

discarded at the first sign of infection

I appreciate anxiety

ways of fixing things for the present

it is a sick joke to make the body most
receptive to things that will kill it

condemned to distraction
compensation
I mean the throw of the dice
I mean never say die
never say the same thing twice

Taking My Breath Away or Points of Entry

I.
some
times

coincident

of meeting like lips

or an open mouth
beneath skin tones
after hushed tones
the inflection
unmistakable spoken
words are puffs of air

after death I kept reading
words returning
returning words

acting them out
trying to get the tone right
multiple copies
breathed in
homeless
estranged in servers
words between bodies
doing their best

and the pure
transmission
of kissing

2.
wander through
small breaths and breathing
I moved my mouth as if in darkness
and wonder
you move through me
like rain
just touching as if
just touching almost
not touching at all fingers
just touching

3.
drawn across by potential difference
exposing nerve endings to cool air
the frayed ends of unfinished business
a working body mechanically lifting
limb upon limb

beneath the surface small anxieties
a sensation of heat in the residue
a dying back of worn flesh

and above the lacerations time purrs
of bodies
expensive as instruments
with nothing certain but the unforeseen
beyond your wildest dreams
things that will take your breath away

4.
I try on different directions
address codes

you are a mail box
why would I stop there?
how can I rest my case?
where is the journey's end?

5.
sternum rises and falls
it indicates breathing or something
beyond that little else
you are double entry

6.
leaning back against the stars
I chatter
deep within the conversation system
locks tumble
open and then closed

between geopolitics I lost track of time
the means of exchange the words

I hold myself dear
I almost touch the keyboard
words fold on the screen
at the point of entry
breaking down
encoded thoughts
work station
generating each sentence
from the smallest propositions

in a hall of mirrors I
go to ground
try to figure it out
where it becomes material
where the flesh kicks in

reconstituted the written words
splash in an empty pool
I leant back and swam in language
pulled every trick in the book
generative, degenerative
through the fire wires
along the line of sentence
whose ending I can only guess at

I can read over and over

in a sentence a pause appears
I insert a comma

I double up
behind the words only
blank paper
behind each letter the
movement outward
from finger tips
tip of the tongue

7.
night has begun to fall
I walk across your shadow step
upon an opening
and the dark spin of the stories
we tell ourselves

in walls, windows, doors
the ground opens
and what can I be certain of

the openings in skin
through which sound escapes

I am inflatable
I am uncoordinated
I am disorganised

8.
in penitent I
drop my head
I hang my shoulders
say mean whiles
a frame between fences paces
become a measure of time
between the walls the numbers
metres per second
I am in penitentiary

I am locked up
I am in hold down
buttoned down
battened down
I am in denial
I am indisputable
I am incapable
I am injured

9.
I cannot organise myself
I remain empty
I reach inside
I feel around inside
down through the
holes in the skin

I move through as if mist
I go through and emerge
gone beyond merger
past the melting point
past curse and cure

and I am defiant and paying
lip service
shuffling the papers off the desk
like eager hands
taking apart my rib cage
my heart

before once more making meaning
from a download
re-casting the words into different shapes
a part from
sectioned
brushing things aside
clear the table
make the bed
dust the house with fine dust
that fills my mouth my nose
I repeat myself
I repeat
I repeat
myself

Sarn Helen

drifting through
implantation the
taste of air
the time
of day the
short and long of it

the moments of
the system behind
the eyes
steps as a necessity
moments of stress
of complications

and when the joints
are oiled as
can be expected
inhabiting the
eyelids the
feet nailed on

landing I take the
body with me as a
source of entertainment
for stroking on long
winter evenings
and shuddering

against moon
light I can't escape
is locked down inside
a me that
matters in the
material a flesh
perspective

might provide the
little windows through
which the sun rises

across the mountains
across the bay
and the three eyed

fish wink to itself at
a joke that has been
doing the
rounds and bowing
out through
curtains of

clouds and before the
outlaws before them
after all
a few shaped stones
arranged into
a taste of history

a bite sized
chunk
that makes little
sense an
impression of the
words

we searched the maps
for tell tale signs
that could trip us up
and our boots
of Spanish leather
and our crockery

on a table of
kindred and affinity
whosoever are
related
are forbidden to
marry together

in bog myrtle

(for Lee Harwood)

sighted down the broken wall to where
a series of valleys from the ridges at the
heads of the valleys agencies

I overlooks
I views
I sights
an aim in life

mountain stand and deliver
before setting off again, swinging a trail leg
the angles were kind of cute
lunch simply
pause between breaths

they should wait until the pears drop or the
orchard reaching out to another in the
silence inhabitants
used lights
as indicators
and could turn either way
eyes might dim
or the advantage point sink without a trace

the sounds rustled across the plain
swept the surface of the lake
as haw and
blackthorn twisted
which trunk was
which myths circulated

standing before the tree and wondering
which sloe or haw
staring down the valley
drawing a line
points of view
the things that get told
you got me there

from this place

A number of connectives
Muscles through flesh to bone
Fat as a thin layer
Wings and arms
And what the fuck does
Understand mean

I buy a house to keep the body warm
Below the thinning shell
Pumping arms to place the air between
Everything in its place a place for
An aid to memory
Liver squeezed dry
Taking away the empties
Too much noise too many
Appointments to be kept
A movement of cell structure
Loud and laughing too loud and laughing
Nothing I could not say
Should have kept quiet
About the blood group

Beating my brow
Slapping my thigh
Taking a hit
Giving a hand
Moving the goalposts

Last night I stayed in
Sparkling
In submission
The book reaching completion
Withdrawn from circulation
And going grey

No Way Back

Sun shifts position
wind from another
quarter blockages
the movement of water
concentration poor or off centre
heart turned over love and
sex the worn rock undercut
a wash from the west

There is no second chance only the
rearrangement of the senses the
pull of the heart sings discordant
across the generations of the things that
move us most; bone, muscle, blood
the desire for the perception
of beauty the desire for the
attainment of beauty

There is no second wind
air moving past or the blow
to the head and catch as catch can
a few words clutched beyond the
point of no return he turns and
disappears as a figure of speech
points to the horizon look at
that

I compose myself a series of
crotchets minims things I could
well do without membership
expired and the aspiration

to fulfil the task of a
better world I arrange
organs of speech clear my
throat begin to say something

The sea drags shingle
over and over the stone in
heaps of stone more smooth
granite pebbles more marble
and what can politics tell me
of the soft landscape
of the body or the hard wiring
of sex or what can landscape

Tell me of the soft politics
of the body of the first
fix the performed
operation as the
memory of a warm body etched
in the soft tissue as it drips
word by word as it
tears itself sentence by

Sentence as it storms
image through dirty image and
the arguments go on in a parody
of logic as if the answer is
buried in the disorganisation
as if once the bits and pieces
of the past are finally slotted
into place or maybe the

Unexamined life is the better
option or the air from an open
window and what can
intelligence tell me I don't
already know as if the tips of
the fingers or the mobile lips
could lie and in confidence here's
the lines from around my eyes

From staring at the setting sun
from a westerly coast where
the rocks in layers lower themselves
into the sea and the guillemots
come and the choughs flash their
legs or the puffins and I'm still
scared to go up high into the
lighthouse still and scared to look back

June 21 2004

A single star and a sickle moon
Bass rise and fall in liquid rings

The smell of honeysuckle

And each becalmed occasion
On approach
The ripples
Each vertebrae
Slips every disc
Displaced

For the hear and now
I was warned by the sound
From the instant it hit the water
The sound of fillet
The whip of spiny backbone

I can almost taste it
Rip the skin
From its fishy body or
Dive underwater
And discover anchorage

The moon goes behind a cloud the
Star disappears through a bank of trees
Mud and water
There is light and then
Lights on the surface

Sea birds the year turns

assumed position

temporarily
across the datum line
to a level
framing a doorway
and a set of assumptions
positions land
reclamation
language as
speech defects
from house to house
a room to breathe

making a series of connections
I missed the last train home
waving from the front door
gales of laughter
as a passing life as a
misconnection
between the thought and the
emotion
in those terms
as the sequence from
location to
articulation
through the luxury of
time passing
or a distance of
perspective
the sequence
became clear from
place to place
in isolation
the daily doorframe
added each day it
wasn't always
like that

one word
after another

words written over
or never even said
except in the head
and what can you do
except accept
the dissolution
except position
yourself
in every camp

there is no problem
reversing

inconstancy is a virtue

the vibration
of distant life forms

no
where no
way left
and left again

One Swallow

1. inhospitable

5 males
3 females
1 cube

next day

3 males 2 females 1 cube

next day

1 male no females no cubes

the ward fills

I set out my table according to my needs
with precision
Collected Poems by Lee Harwood
a notebook (this one)
a pen
a milkshake
discover
there is nothing more important than to swallow

I swallowed the whole story
beginning, middle and end
chew for hours sometimes and forget to swallow
I keep talking
the outer and the inner become divided
I never knew pain that couldn't be killed off
if properly approached
I went in the back way
stealthily
not the how but the why
the rhythm of institutional life
why I look this way
nothing nor pale broth

2. hospitality suite

the love of meaning

night became disturbed

two bodies shift a little closer
across the time of separation
and two bodies that have filtered maybe or
strained maybe trying to take care

sand wears ever smaller
bodies turn to dust
wearing off the edges
creating resistance
and most of all the smell
breaking down
the distance
between bodies

3. necking

as an entrance and when it swells
the epiglottis and the oesophagus
get blocked
the other holes
more ways out than in
except for the stigmata
on the back of the hand
and at the joint of the elbow
as replacements for oral transmission
through the medium of air
fluids mingle

penetration is open to question
caked with dried blood
and what does infection mean
how is a structure changed
does the end of the pipe bend over?
I never remember being so aware of
internal organs
I remember eating andouilette
I remember holding the tail of a rat
I could neither spit nor swallow
I make a note (this note) to look up the word infection

I realise bacteria
release germ warfare
and patient and waiting to be
hooked up to the bags
a nurse sat by the bed
I couldn't sleep

I dreamt of food
of roast duck, which I never eat,
of scrambled eggs
before things could happen
or the succession of events up to an
apprehension

4. theatre of dreams

bringing hospitality to the theatre
learning welcoming skills
front of house
hoping to move on in order
like food sliding down, soup, meat, pudding

took me years to learn the symptoms
an odd person who invaded all available space
past the bones in the nose even the
small cavities
flooding with fibre optic light exposing
pink flesh

this incessant desire to fill page after page with words
to love, to reach, to control

5. dream on

shifting, settling, changing
over time like sediment
in blood

and then it settles at all points into
each other molecules settling
into each other

same hair same eyes cells falling
into each other settling sliding off

settling over time same hair falling
impossible velocity

6. shining light

never too rich or too thin
it is an irony that
those things that damage it most my body
which now refuses food has
welcomed with open arms

Toe Nail

(close up of toe-nail)

organic marine matter

receding into the distance

pier end

(coming up all too fast)

pale sunlight

water fronting

pier ending

sun shining nigh

unto the end

pier pressure

everyone out – knocking down

these doors – drowning

the same circles

take a break eat
take the third roundabout
and feeling as if only or impossible
desire imagined medinas cool air off
the atlas the geography of a new country
the trip was taking me out of myself and then
what was left? inserting the endless
possibilities from casual to smart
casual and exhausted I blew
myself out

in the airport that is a city
names get mangled
ah david sōn
in the north terminal
names becoming mangled
in the place that becomes a city
through commerce
all points of the compass
I flew south
little left over

there are no maps of the medina
the people are many times restored
bodies carpets tattoos
reversible skin
inside out
live stock
boiled to dish rags
hand maiden

the way the connections of a real life never end unlike the closed world of
a fiction expressed in a few hundred pages and maybe that's why the price
of real life or the cost of living is shocking beyond belief

narratives close in
double knotted
making good siesta
the silence of the hooves

streets opening out into other streets many
ways to construct the medina
many ways to live a life
doorways within doorways up stairs
the recycled treads of the horses hooves

blue cobalt blue indigo blue incomplete
upper stories the silk yarns like
broken threads or a completed
building lacks a roof in certain
quarters the overspill in the mosque
canalised Idriss founder of Fez like a snagged
tooth stumbling over the Arabic
from holding it all in

wave upon wave
what is it to make of it all
holding it all in
digging into absorption
walking out on history
pretty mosaics and many of them
many pointed stars
doorways shaped like keyholes
multiple stomach disorders
gardens in symmetry disordered
minds and in winter sunshine
the crusade is to wipe Islam
off the face of the earth
until every smile is wiped off
every Arab face until
every corner of public space
is marked private and has a cost attached

he greets his friends warmly his
hand held between two hands he
touches his chest and takes away the
arm in a gesture of such gentleness
the bird bound hand and foot

it was a reflecting pool deep in the socket of the skull

intense privilege
real beauty
for the elite
by the end of the day
living without foundation
on the surface of Islam

sincerity
love
denial

adherence
knowledge
certainty

acceptance
compliance
truthfulness

key incidents

walking through doorways
following the mosque the minarets

I observed all of real life
stroked my arm
went to town
in a wonderful world and
approaching the bar
what idea might I hold for more than a minute
that truth might be stranger
than the limited framework of fiction
the endless possibilities
unfolding into the future
coming up from the past
linked across continents

this might give meaning to the trip
the things left undone and remain undone
a tectonic plate flies loose
at the point where words fail me
in alphabet soup
sweeping through the lower intestine
the last man standing up to be counted
against the adding machine
the final sum
by the time a
certain age is reached
what time she went to bed
and mainly Morrocans
drinking
elevating the limb
a repeated custom
until the difficult becomes
easy to achieve
or the idea that every
land is fundamentally different

I make snap judgements
a pair of aces
a pain in the neck
could be cancer of course
or a particularly aggressive infection
impossible to escape
history like a clanking sack of discarded items
limping away from his own history
dragging a leg

the body resisting in every point of
viral contact every gland swollen
the only worthwhile thing is the
struggle to pull out
one foot then the
other there is no new space

no new man

no new poetry

a lumber yard for a brain
and a wooden leg that taps out a
genetic code the tat that is
the constructed life style
the fabrication of different
contexts differing marginally

searching his face for his own history
(rejuvenating)
no way back
no way out
no controls
no freedom

patterns accumulate against what we would be
pools for fishing behind the eye
blood darkening the brain
headlong rush into darkness
somebody pulled
the switch
on neural download or plug in

connections just aren't there
the roads not yet built
the way not paved
the numbers beyond calaculation
as was the weather not to be
counted on little left over

Out of Sight

there are no borders to
the conversation
I can have with myself

any subject that
comes up
hey
I'm an expert
in monkey business
although

feeling more or less
alone
in the monkey business
there were
no time limits
beyond the circulation of blood
and

right the

endless word to the
next word
until a line might
come stepping out
and take me by the hand

right

into remaining time
at the end of the line
what's left over
what you want
the bit left
over
a remainder right
a combinatory
the commiseration
right

had a dream last night
upside down in a canoe
Joni Mitchell was in the
dream
women will be the death of me

getting beyond
things going wrong
no sense to it
without intelligence
or a private income

blue
blue

right – this is a hazard
awareness test
and I'm too slow
there are
police on the streets
open laughing buckets
of white wine open
to the air and
the unexpected
below a certain
depth
below a certain level of
engagement
out of nothing
out of nothing from out of

girl's laugh
girls
drifting on annual
contracts
missing drifting
lost inaction hands simply
not responding

and I slash and burn
move from one job to the next
the links falling away behind me

oh the world as it is, now

oh misinformed materialisms
foolish attempt at explanations

right

making claims to accuracy based on ...
making claims of comprehension

pick, pick away then mix

that's what works
in the centre writing and places
you never wanted to go
the places where a life turns
links dissolve the
silver threads snap
the range of vision
is taken out of the comfort
zone I can show you

right

I can invalidate any claim
how good is that
I can demonstrate meaninglessness
how good is that

my apologies
and I'm sorry
but I'm keen to know
what it all might mean

maybe language is not a fit medium
maybe poetry is not a fit medium

maybe its only the body
circulating blood
losing its grip
beyond kin or kind
how it got there
how it is
what it is
this side
that side
notes that
might become how
low how low

right

Dream Boat

The turquoise swell of the sea of dreams
As if all the dreams of the turquoise ship

I am the man of my dreams
Endless features repeat themselves
Mountains falling into the sea
A peninsula floating on reflected light

And I can almost smell you the man of
My dreams the swirling currents
The depths no one can touch
Seagulls sleeping on the swell
The long flight for scraps keeping pace
With the lingering touch of the ship
On the surface of the sea

I have no doubts I am the man of my dreams
The buoys that never get to shore the boys
And who could resist who
Never seem too sure the sea of dreams the
Swim of birds for scraps the sleep of
Birds on the sea's surface rocking

spending time

honesty
not worth the effort
clarity
over-rated

like a beached whale
any structure must be untrustworthy
any superstructure shored up

play is foolish (natch)
the body left
linked to the body
right
whatever I'm living
in
the passage of time
along a path of least resistance
down the slippery slope

the magic carpet curls up
feet begin to twitch
the shuttle flying
between levers

a life rich in the growing
trends in tapestry
pelmets for the body's
furniture
as the power of water
from the heavy clouds
the dark hills
the table cloth on which
the nation feeds
in golden hands
I mean lands
beyond reparation
slippery slopes

taking my fate in my hands

Bangor July 2005

a poem beginning

the town

is too quiet

and out of the

question

the town disappears

over the horizon

the brow of an eye

or a thin girl

shovelling in

chocolate bars

a packet of papers

a packet of straight cigarettes

too much

sugar rush too little distance for a

mind to travel on the

tip of at the back

of my mind

at the forefront of

thinking how far can a

mind how far for have a

care for the mind to travel

it is quiet in town for thinking

for linking words by the way they sound

from whatever part of a past

whatever hard wiring

the soft palate tasting each

syllable and I repeat myself

beaches

blue

islands

this is a poem to fill space left

over between the fore word and the

after word this poem has no links to any

other poem or anything that might

exist outside the poem it is simply

something that lasts from its beginning

to its end and where a poem should go

do you know what I mean?

with one ear to the ground for the approaching train

I'm sick of politics for example

I'm sick of Blair being in a poem

for example

I'm sick of Bush being in a poem

the poem is a space to move around in

I don't want them cluttering up the place

engaging me in conversation

telling me how tough their work is

a poem is a place for thinking

with one good ear to the wall my eyes

glued my fingers locked rehearsing

if only I'd said this or that or known

what might go wrong before it

goes wrong

I'm sick of to the back

teeth of reflective

practice thinking

about the things

that have already gone wrong

that can't get put right and still

thinking about them

as I talk into the space the poem has made

and the space the poem is left the town

is quiet tonight

and my own words seem to shine

under the lights

with an eye to the future

the sensation

of being go-between

the paper and the pen the moving

hand rolls cigarettes the pen

lies as water after the storm has been

and abstracting the sense of

something or other

And I'm scared in town

of falling in love

at first sight

my heart sinks from

the fear

of going down

at first sight

shot down in flames

love is a trial to me

love is a sentence

love in the space of endless possibility

between the first and second drink

when all the threads can be gathered up

it is quiet in town tonight

In order 2

One foot after an other an
other one foot after

Another and then the
other foot after another

Heart beat

That's an order

The mechanics of
Biology
The curve of melancholy

That's in order

Foot fall
Skin care

Skipping a beat

How do you know what
You don't know

What order is knowledge in

Send out the skin for a
Walk for the day
To see what it might find

Wet rain
Walking to the beating pulse
Heart rate rising
Hips stiffening
To order
Fries

A Moment 2

I suppose it's the passage of time
and the way it folds fore and aft or

takes an unexpected turn
the boat was an inflatable full of air

it broke its plywood back on a wave
this seems to be a moment

to go forward or back when
the scales of time

hah

are tipping towards the future
I examined the weight of evidence

became distracted forgetting
this is a summer of love and hate

when anger turns on a misplaced word
whinging about the housework

and getting fat
surfing waves of feeling

keeping away from dry land
riding the route of cycle

signs of life

between wit and reason
action and indifference
nervous impulses
anxious rushes of
emotion across the
table across the
spread pages of a
game when I had to
ignore all
intelligence all
information the signs
were all there on the
page spread out and
collapsing under stress

damped down the page
curled into a foetal
position hiding all signs
of life, you know, the
little ones, breathing,
a beating heart a pin
jabbed at a foot just
out of the womb the
long skinny leg a
pin jabbed into the
foot until he cried
well that's life for you

Making Up

The thing about the past is it's never clear where it all began;
different dates, chance meetings, cancelled appointments a
biologically determined dress code signals that simply passed by
unnoticed or indifferently given. I have no present for our

anniversary only a hole to dig yourself out of or a free
pass into uncertainty. There were a number of opportunities
but they were limited in number. Maybe one or two. There
were free rides, lunches that never got paid for that might have

led to something or maybe not. It was as if, or the way a day
never turns out all day light or all cloud cover how there are
chinks and turns. A matter of sufficient physical mobility
whether clearing a low doorway or avoiding oncoming

traffic. That is indisputable. No argument. A slender waist
and a mobile tongue can keep the wolf from the door and
gain entry into the professions. Beyond reach. Can't be
pinned down. Where the only choice is to take the knife

to your unruly skin and cause damage where it is least
expected. The people who tell lies recognise each
other and their only desire is to stop the devious
circuitry of their own half remembered

history and arrive at a moment where the future can be
spread out from the certainty of the past or the present
explanations hold water. I choose the treadmill, pumping
out of the hold and the eternal bleed wells working in relief.

Between ethnicity and the exotic I want more exotic.
I want to be taken out of myself.
I want to want. I want to don't want to want. To don't want.
The thing is what I want is not clear the past spread out.

The Independent

When people in a tube train look
anxiously around at other people on a
tube train. When all the scraps
of litter have been cleared the discarded
bits and pieces of urban life. When the
scaffolding goes up and the
polythene sheets go round
and the journalists sit in a pen in the
middle of the road their cameras on tripods
just waiting and waiting. This is no time to
play with words. This is a time
for plain speaking.
Like these bombs are not connected
to the invasion of Iraq.
That's plain speaking.
That gets to the heart of the matter.
And I know in order to be clear
I have to tell lies or at least strip so
many of the difficulties away there is nothing
worth anything left as if the bare truth is no
truth at all and to get to the heart of the matter
is to discard all matter that matters and once the
difficulties in explaining almost anything
become the difficulty then that's when
the difficulty of the situation is explored.
See what I mean? This is hard.

A number of conflicting emotions
which refuse to consolidate.
Or even incomprehension.
That would be good. I cannot comprehend.
I wish I could say that and mean it. You cause
a war on someone's soil and then they bring
a bit of it back to yours. How hard is that to
comprehend? But then again, shrinking into
myself in a tube train. In that confined place
with all those people. How to speak plainly
of that or even think it in any way other
than in language that cannot contain it.

There is no position I can hold for more
than a moment and the wind from an
approaching train pushes me up and
out of the tube into the hot street
and the names of the streets and the
faces of the people and I cannot
take it all in or give it out.

There is no single perspective but on
bended knee or on all fours or the view
from above as if there is a thing called justice.
As if there might be neutral ground
from which this could be
understood or called to account or
any system or any due process or twelve
good men and true. The apostles bore witness.
The judge walks on water. A judgement is final.

a little light industry

in the smoothed over surface
little sign of the weather
in the stainless skin
clogged pores
trowelled in

no hand in the matter
and hard to read the past
the hollows
as shafts of air I read
as air pushed hard until it
pants and falls or
brushed into neat piles

through regeneration
the earth is covered
with a contemporary skin
which can barely conceal
at its outer edges
a waste ground the
commodified surface
tries to overwrite
the lank grass half
dead the brown field site
crawling with toxins
and secure parking

the glass is floor to ceiling
the hardwood floor is beech
the splash back stainless

I want the wet room
the power shower
where I would
never grow old
and from the brushed
aluminium spatter the
surface of the quayside
each wrinkle regenerated

plastered over re-
newed dis
placed

no history of the material
but an endless what
might it mean
and an impossible
dream of renewal
of the cells realignment

The Guantánamo Resort

she said the memory was in the place.
although that might have been face
and the key identifier. fobbed off with

a square peg in a lock barrel a
tenon without a mortice a lever with
out an enzyme or even an incorrect

substrate. unless an induced fit
by filing down teeth or grinding the
molars. there is no lock and key only

a number pad on which to play variations
discover off key moments until the
body parts click together or the tumblers

and their homing devices fly into an
empty cage and begin to make a home.
they had no memory of where they'd

been, the tumblers, or any sense of face
recognition. leave home. and by your
leave. absent without leave. leave it.

moon and mist matters

history: the
impossibility of
movement: weight
cannot be clicked

on and off collecting
people from the
beyond and spreading
them thin as a scrape

on the surface as if
the luck or the bad cells
run wild in the night
might rub off: but for

now it's good
bye folding back
deep into the brain
last spark of the

synapse final
flutter of the eye
I glanced across
occasionally

I saw it coming
the moon parts the clouds
a thin chemical taste
the blood orange full moon

the mist across the moon
a feeling of freedom
the road rushing from
me from tide and time

into pooling dark matter
and uncertainty a
pause in proceedings
potential differences

waveform

from the waveform beneath the skin
in the early stages and before a prognosis
it was after all a Wednesday

a body will let you down when least
expected the currents suddenly
privatised as the memory full
to bursting is ready to roll a black
out and a thrown switch

if the expression is clear
if the milk of human kindness
can run freely another
temporary medium like easy street
or budget airlines and on a higher
plane the toxins spreading
like a series of secondaries

I ride international
clinging on the tail
of the tumour
as a meeting place
or crossing the wake in
the lymphatic and
whatever the deal
deal with it
however the deck
stacks or the cards
riffling through the air
and flying, to keep the
hammer down to turn the
wheel to feel the cool spray

Calling

I don't remember things
anymore what they are
or what they do only what
they look like or what they

are called and anyway they
change over time the built
structures drooping
and paint peeling

I do remember injustice
 it was easy and she re-
called her past the mem
ories that made her

privileged and all I
don't know I
do remember a lack of
material goods I still lack

material goods or
stopping the flow
a gob stopper
the curling wave

of a wall of words
the eye picks out
a name from a mess
of names calling

to them across time
and badly treated
etched into the wall
of words and fading

over time the indentations
filling with grit or grown
over and the shades and
shadows still scratching

their names and then
rubbed out it is as if
the name stood for
anything sig

nificant or the
code could be
traced back to the
moment of
its conception or
growth had a
single source a

river a first
raindrop that gathered
along the branch that
dropped into its path

a ready made gully
whose gently guiding
banks keep the straight
and narrow a lake has

little memory
of the drops of rain that
losing shape
or linking up

Seas of flags

Coconut smell of
Warm gorse
Cream blossom
Of late haw

Ducks take off and land
A dog across a fence like a
Seal a flock of geese

The water diverting
The family a unit

between mess and message

walking the streets with a dead
bird cradled in his hands
not always fully dressed

he would arrange matches around the
bed to trip up any in
truders or dislocate mischief

makers he carried a hatchet on

special occasions

laying down in the road for no
apparent reason the
car went over him and killed him

it could be that quick
and for no apparent reason
so sudden and for no apparent
cause

they hung speakers from the upstairs
windows so they rattled the glass of
the flat below to drive him crazy

that was a slow process but effective

the random nature of sudden death
the slow progress of terminal illness
the accident of accident of nonsense
of mental illness that eats away at the
corners of the room and lets in anything

a world gone mad and where sense
flies out through the window there is
no sleep that can cure bad dreams
no cure for too many meaningless words

switching codes

and I remember killing
time in a town that
never seemed to get going
peering in at a shop window
at the cost of living
and its accessories

the bits around the edges
all those hidden extras
days full of light and dark
a clocked face coming out of
shadows repeatedly a failure
to properly lock the door
to turn out the cat put out
the gas empty my mind my heart

bore hole

the feeling of
scar tissue sewn
up too
loose
tattooed on
the bodies of
indigenous whites
the drift to the
inside against
the camber
simple gesture of
elbow no-one
alone with a table
no convers
ation no dis
agreement

eyes begin to close head
to nod
that would never do
upset
drunk

I remember a pale imitation of who you were or what you might become

falling away
peeling off from the sand
the way you flick your hair
the walk of shame
our self delusion or
determination
rising to the challenge
my sons
my brothers
lovers

fish, flesh and fowl

Puffyn a fysshe lyke a teele

with its short wings
the puffin
is hardly a bird at all

*Puffins, whom I may call the feathered fishes, are accounted even by the holy
fatherhood of Cardinals to be no flesh but rather fish*

it tastes of sand eels
is confused with the razor bill
the guillemot
the young shearwater

Puffins, Birdes less then Dukkes having grey Fethers like Dukkes

caught by a gust it can
rise like air the puffin
eaten during lent as a
matter of convenience

*The Puffyn . . . whose young ones are thence ferretted out, being exceeding fat, kept
salted, and reputed for fish, as comming neerest thereto in their taste*

*or a sort of Coot or Seagull, supposed to be so called from its round belly; as it were
swelling and puffing out.*

*Known by the fishermen as sea parrots or coulternebs; but more generally designated
in books as puffins.*

the bill was neither
large nor coloured the key
identifier of a puffin as I tried
to weave a story like the
steps that wind inside the
lighthouse as the story rose

I have twenty lambs . . . as plump as puffins.

increasingly insecure
and feeling the vertigo of a
lack of accuracy there
were spots of rain an island
view the setting sun

under cloud cover I leant
on the bar talked about
myself a subject as
constructed as if there is no
relationship between the words
and anything else as a puffin
turns out to be a guillemot or a
razor bill or a bird is a fish for lent

and what is in the name whether
the short bird puffs to itself at the
speed of its wings or its puffed
out beak a delicacy and tasting
of the fish it lives on and the
puffing sound it makes a short
growl or laugh but all these are
unlikely conjecture and based
on insecure grounds

language can only take you so far
sometimes you have to step out
sometimes you have to quieten the
jangle of nerves connect the
inside and outside or link
skin onto skin the loose ends
of being alive and waiting for a
connection I went to the old places
and walked them around again
places too familiar for words

www.ingramcontent.com/pod-product-compliance
Lightning Source LLC
Chambersburg PA
CBHW022201080426
42734CB00006B/533